SPOKEN WORD, SET IN MOTION
POETRY SERIES

IN RESPONSE TO LIFE

Booklet of Poetry, vol II

JERRY RIZZI

ISBN: 979-8-89704-804-5 (Paperback)

[CREDITS]

Graphic Design/Editing by Becky Durante
Images & Photographs:
Front & Back Cover Images by Helena Jeppson
Photographs/Artwork for:
Poem II by Becky Durante & Regina Dowker
Poems I; III-XIV by Becky Durante
Poems XV-XVI by Regina Dowker
Poem XVII, XVIII by Jerry Rizzi

Special thanks to the Pexels & Pixabay Photography Communities for providing a variety of images for modification and inspiration in this book.
(www.pexels.com; www.pixabay.com)

Self-Published by Author.
Printed and bound in the United State of America
First Printing January, 2025

Dedication

As with any of my writings, be it poetry or music, I want to thank my immediate family for their support and encouragement.

I love them with all my heart.

My Beautiful Daughter Christina

My Son Benjamin

My Son Anthony

My Beautiful Granddaughter Rose

CONTENTS

I – WAKENED DREAMS

A pasture of echoes
Ever present, into the Night
and back into Daylight
Familiar Settings, Roads once Taken
Familiar faces that reappear

A Pasture of contemplations
Speculations of things to come,
Roads not yet Taken
With a variance of
Wonderment, Enchantment
Uncertainty, Enlightenment

Eyes closed
Eyes wide open
Wakened Dreams

II – THE COMMON TONE IN THE JOURNEY OF MUSIC

In the Journey of a music Composition
A common tone will have
a Myriad of Expressive sounds
Melodious-Harmonious-Dissonant
All throughout an entire scorebec
At times one may standout more notably

And while we are all on our journey in this world
We are each a common tone in
"God's Song of Life"

III – SHADOW

Casting a shadow of doubt
Hidden within a mindset
With or without rays of light
Be it day or night

Once it is spoken out
A Shadow reflecting
the thoughts and words
Are No longer hidden

Though soon would fade away
With diminishing Rays of light
And dimming lights at night
Back into The Hidden Mindset

Casting a shadow of doubt

IV – CITY SKETCHES

Picturesque
Captivating
Skyscrapers
Designing & Defining
The City Skyline
Creating a Rustic Setting
In Black & White
Invoking Reactions
Curiosity and Admiration by many afar
Familiarity to others that have visited
Nostalgia expressed by those
Who once were residents
Meaningful to the many
That do indeed reside
Within The

City Sketches

V – TIME SENSITIVE

Waiting for tomorrow
While living yesterday
Today never arrives
And as it continues,
Metaphorically
At the blink of an eye
Time slips by, to a shortened week
And yet for an other with the same
Initial scenario, time stood still
Creating a long - lengthened week
Though either way, in the end
Like the wings on a bird, time flies
"Time Sensitive Material"

VI – THE ART OF SOMETIMES

Sometimes taking a step Back
May be the prerequisite
To putting the Best Foot Forward
With a new direction
And or
A renewed=altered current path

And yes reevaluating
With mixed emotion
Sometimes taking a step Back
May become the First Step Forward

VII – THE NOCTURNAL NIGHT OWL WITHIN

Hints of being Nocturnal
Indeed, a Night Owl
Is in Place
Daylight begins with a yawn
No time for naps
A rather full day ahead
With a busy roadmap
And when finally
the day comes to an end
Dusk to Dawn begins
Once again Harkening back

To That Nocturnal Night Owl within

VIII. THE NARRATIVE

From the beginning of a new day
To the days end
A Narrative in Place
Be it ordinary insignificant
Unusual extraordinary
Agreements Disagreements
All Become engaging conversations
Some may be in silence
though still be heart-felt
A Collective of Narratives
Daily routines in Life

IX. MEMOIRS

On any given day
Be it lonely & quiet
While reminiscing
Be it rather Busy & Brisk
With things in place
And things out of sorts
Yet All are worthy of memoirs
Perspectives and Reflections
Past and present
Indeed
Memoirs throughout life
float in the air, Drifting
into the Skies Above
Past and Present

Memoirs

X. PAST & PRESENT

The distant Past
May feel like it is right
 around the corner
And in many an instance
Indeed, it is

While a recent past
may have a feel
of distance and far gone

Either Recent or distant Pasts
Live within the Presence
of thy mind

XI. SEQUENTIAL ELEMENTS

When What is now

Becomes what once was

Then What is to come has arrived

Encompassing and Nurturing

Man & Nature itself

Unforeseen & Relinquishing

Expectations & Embracing

Sequential Elements in the

Pathway of Life

XII. FOREST BOUND

A collective of trees
With limbs reaching out
Creating a tunneled pathway
Paving the way for a
Hiker's Journey
Various animals of the woods may be
seen or heard in the rustling of
bushes
Vestiges of fallen
Leaves & Twigs Throughout
Scattered Shrubs on the Forest Edge
All in Nature's
Earth-Tone Rustic Setting
The Forest

XIII. STRUCTURAL ENGINEERING

With Structural Engineering providing accomplished
works of art
Creating a safety net as it were
For many aspects of brick & mortar

It Is worthy of emulating
One's own structural -Design
Concentrating and accomplishing
In the building blocks
With Many Aspects
Working out previous, current and future
Structures throughout one's life
especially with Family

XIV. HASTENED

At times Hastened to smile
Hesitant to reveal hidden true feelings
slightly Portraying
All is well
Though with no real eye contact
Eventually Privacy elevates to introverted
Like a lone wolf
Like a lone soldier
Fighting a battle
within oneself
While walking down a quiet
country road
And or walking down a busy city sidewalk

Hastened to Smile

XV. INS AND OUTS OF SELF-WORTH

Blinded by $$ Signs
Selfies Taken
While ignoring the inner self
Possessions
Building one's sense of Value
Continuingly Depending on
what others Think
Though
Recognizing providing and sharing
Love and caring
To Family & friends
At times Even to strangers
Just May be the
True Self-Worth

XVI– LEAVES ON A TREE, STAIRCASE OF LIFE

With a rather gentle breeze
Leaves on a Tree lightly Wavering
Create a picturesque setting
On any given day
Ups and Downs may occur
As leaves on a Tree are
Flourishing, Rustling in a strong Wind
Begin to let go, Drifting and Rising
Toward the Skies
While some leaves are
Quickened to fall to the Earth Below
And on any given day, Our Own
Ups and Downs indeed may occur
Within the Spiral Staircase of Life

XVII– IN A CELESTIAL STATE OF MIND

In a Celestial state of mind

Standing on solid ground

In an open field

Eyes staring up into the sky

Amongst a Cascade of clouds

The Sun still peeking through

Aa a Belief system is in place

In a Celestial State of Mind

XVIII– SCENARIO

Jerry Rizzi

I. Scenario

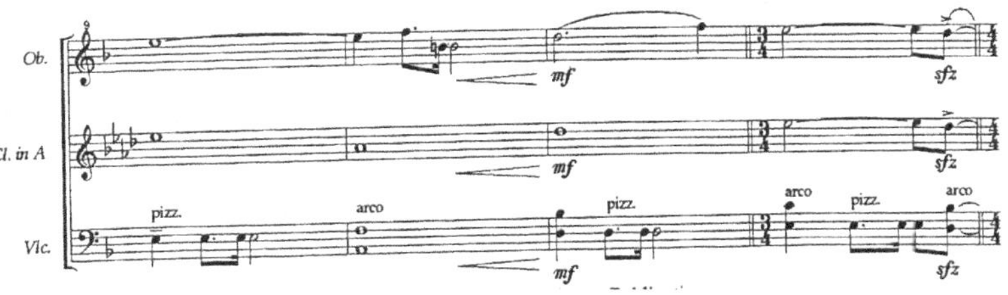

Ob.
Cl. in A
Vlc.
pizz.
arco
mf
mp
Moderato (♩108)
f
3
pizz.
arco
dolce
mf

Ob.
Cl. in A
Vlc.
3
tr
f
ff
mf
mp
Andante (♩= 80)
pizz.
arco

Epilogue

Life is

A Story to be told.
A Poem to be recited.
A Song to be sung.
A Painting to be Framed.

All Intertwined

Acknowledgements

I want to thank the following people for contributing to the creative process:

To my son, Bengamin for helping with the working title, "Structural Design" and phrases.

To Helena Jeppson for her photographic talents in the cover photo

To Regina Dowker for creative artwork,
"The Common Tones in the Journey of Life"
"Ins and outs of Self-worth" and
"Leaves on a Tree, Staircase of Life"
To Becky Durante for contributing graphic designs, pictures, editing and valued feedback.

Made in the USA

Made in the USA
Coppell, TX
29 April 2025

48826396R00030